Boston

Boston

A Downtown America Book

Ingrid Monke

Dillon Press, Inc. Minneapolis, MN 55415

The photographs are reproduced through the courtesy of the Boston Red Sox; the Christian Science Publishing Society of the First Church of Christ, Scientist; Robert Davis; Susan Lapides, the Massachusetts Office of Travel and Tourism; Dave Millert/Tom Stack and Associates; the Museum of Science; and the New England Aquarium. Cover photo by Susan Lapides.

Library of Congress Cataloging-in-Publication Data

Monke, Ingrid.
Boston / by Ingrid Monke.
(A Downtown America book)
Includes index.
Summary: Explores the city of Boston, both past and present, describing neighborhoods, attractions, festivals, and historic sites.
1. Boston (Mass.)—Juvenile literature. [1. Boston (Mass.)]
I. Title. II. Series.
F73.33.M66 1988   974.4'61   88-20202
ISBN 0-87518-382-4

Dillon Press, Inc., 242 Portland Avenue South
Minneapolis, Minnesota 55415

Printed in the United States of America
1 2 3 4 5 6 7 8 9 10 97 96 95 94 93 92 91 90 89 88

Contents

Fast Facts about Boston

Boston: Capital of Massachusetts; Suffolk County Seat; The Hub; Athens of America; Beantown; "Cradle of Liberty"

Location: Atlantic Coast, northeastern Massachusetts

Area: City, 45.4 square miles (117.6 square kilometers); consolidated metropolitan area, 3,035 miles (7,861 square kilometers)

Population (1986 estimate*): City, 573,600; consolidated metropolitan area, 4,055,700

Major Population Groups: Blacks, Irish, Italians, Canadians

Altitude: 21 feet (6.4 meters) above sea level in the downtown area

Climate: Average temperature is 30°F (-1°C) in January, 74°F (23.3°C) in July; average annual precipitation, including rain and snow, is 43 inches (107.5 centimeters)

Founding Date: 1630, chartered as a city in 1822

City Flag: Gold border around a blue flag with the city seal

City Seal: View of the skyline of Boston as it looked in 1822; bears the motto "God Be with Us, as He Was with Our Fathers" in Latin

Form of Government: The mayor is elected for four years and heads the city government. A nine-member city council is elected to two-year terms and passes laws.

Important Industries: Electronics equipment, machinery, printing and publishing, processed foods, seafood, clothing

*U.S. Bureau of the Census 1988 population estimates available in fall 1989; official 1990 census figures available in 1991-92.

Festivals and Parades:

January: Japanese New Year Festival; Chinese New Year

February: New England Boat Show; Frederick Douglass Day

March: *Boston Globe* Jazz Festival; New England Spring Garden and Flower Show; Evacuation Day Parade

April: Great Boston Egg Race; Boston Marathon; Patriot's Day, including Lantern Reenactment, Paul Revere's Ride Reenactment

May: Art Newbury Street; Lilac Sunday at Arnold Arboretum; Beacon Hill Garden Tour; Memorial Day Parade

June: Cambridge River Festival; Ancient & Honorable Artillery Company Parade; Back Bay Street Fair; Landing Day; St. Anthony's Feast Day; Boston Common Dairy Festival; Bunker Hill Day

July: Fourth of July Celebrations, including reading of the Declaration of Independence, USS *Constitution* turnaround, and Boston Pops concert and fireworks; Bastille Day

August: North End Italian festivals; August Moon Festival; Caribbean Carnival Festival

October: Bonne Bell 10K Road Race; Head of the Charles Regatta

November: Veterans Day Parade

December: Christmas tree lighting at Prudential Center; Tea Party Reenactment; First Night Celebration

For further information about festivals and parades, see agencies listed on page 56.

United States

CANADA

WASHINGTON
Seattle
Olympia
Portland
Salem
OREGON

MONTANA
Helena

IDAHO
Boise

NORTH DAKOTA
Bismarck

SOUTH DAKOTA
Pierre

MINNESOTA
WISCONSIN
Lake Superior
St. Paul
Minneapolis
Madison
Milwaukee

Lake Michigan
Lake Huron
MICHIGAN
Lansing
Detroit

Lake Ontario
Lake Erie
NEW YORK
Albany

NEW HAMPSHIRE
VERMONT
MAINE
Montpelier
Concord
Augusta
MASSACH
Boston
Providence
RHODE IS
Hartford
CONNECTIC

WYOMING
Cheyenne

Great Salt Lake
Salt Lake City
UTAH

Carson City
NEVADA

Sacramento
San Francisco

CALIFORNIA

Las Vegas

Los Angeles
San Diego

Denver
COLORADO

NEBRASKA
Omaha
Lincoln

IOWA
Des Moines
Mississippi

ILLINOIS
Chicago
Springfield

INDIANA
Indianapolis

OHIO
Cleveland
Columbus
Cincinnati

Pittsburgh
PENNSYLVANIA
Harrisburg

Trenton
New York City
NEW JERSE
Philadelphia
Dover
DELAWARE
Baltimore
Annapolis
Washington, D.C.
MARYLAND

WEST VIRGINIA
Charleston
Richmond
VIRGINIA

KANSAS
Topeka
Kansas City
Jefferson City
St. Louis
MISSOURI

Louisville
Frankfort
KENTUCKY

ARIZONA
Phoenix
Tucson

Albuquerque
Santa Fe
NEW MEXICO

El Paso

Tulsa
Oklahoma City
OKLAHOMA

ARKANSAS
Little Rock

Memphis
TENNESSEE
Nashville

NORTH CAROLINA
Raleigh
Charlotte
Columbia
SOUTH CAROLINA

Fort Worth
Dallas

TEXAS

San Antonio
Austin
Houston

Rio Grande

Baton Rouge
LOUISIANA
New Orleans

Jackson
MISSISSIPPI

Birmingham
Montgomery
ALABAMA

Atlanta
GEORGIA

Tallahassee
Jacksonville

St. Petersburg
Tampa
FLORIDA
Miami

Pacific Ocean

Atlantic Ocean

MEXICO

Gulf of Mexico

U.S.S.R.

ALASKA
Anchorage
Juneau

CANADA

Honolulu
HAWAII

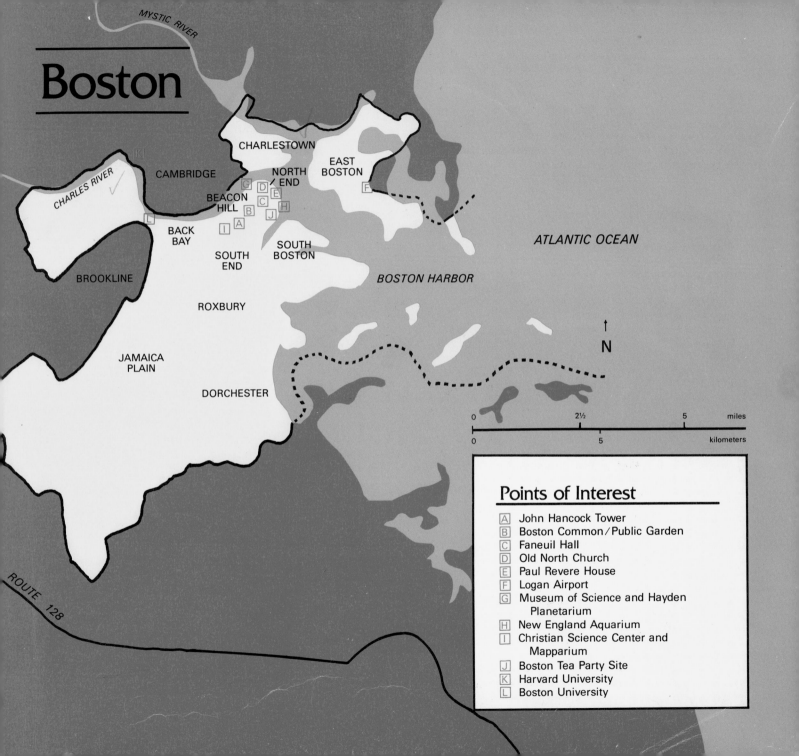

Boston

MYSTIC RIVER

CHARLESTOWN

CAMBRIDGE

NORTH
END

EAST
BOSTON

CHARLES RIVER

BEACON
HILL

BACK
BAY

SOUTH
END

SOUTH
BOSTON

BROOKLINE

ROXBURY

JAMAICA
PLAIN

DORCHESTER

ATLANTIC OCEAN

BOSTON HARBOR

N

ROUTE 128

| 0 | 2½ | 5 | miles |
| 0 | | 5 | kilometers |

Points of Interest

- A John Hancock Tower
- B Boston Common/Public Garden
- C Faneuil Hall
- D Old North Church
- E Paul Revere House
- F Logan Airport
- G Museum of Science and Hayden Planetarium
- H New England Aquarium
- I Christian Science Center and Mapparium
- J Boston Tea Party Site
- K Harvard University
- L Boston University

1

Boston:
"Hub of the Universe"

What do Paul Revere, Harvard University, the Polaroid company, and the Red Sox have in common? All of them belong to Boston, the largest city in New England and the capital of Massachusetts. Boston is a historic city, more than 350 years old, whose citizens are proud of its traditions. Yet it is also a modern city, a center for education and research, and the home of many of the country's top comput-

er companies. It's a hustling, bustling place, squeezed onto a small piece of land.

Boston seems crowded today, hemmed in by rivers and its Atlantic coast harbor. The Mystic River flows from the north, and the Charles River from the west. Boston Harbor, dotted with islands, lies to the east. More than fifteen bridges span the waterways. The biggest one, Tobin Bridge,

Downtown Boston viewed from the Charles River.

In Boston's harbor, big freighters unload their cargo.

stretches high across the Mystic River.

Boston is one of the biggest ports on the Atlantic Ocean, and the sea has always played an important role in its history. In the days before trucks and airplanes could transport goods, people depended on the sea for fishing and trading. Today the harbor still buzzes with activity. Warehouses and docks, hotels, condominiums, and office buildings line the shore. Tugboats guide big freighters in past small sailboats to unload their

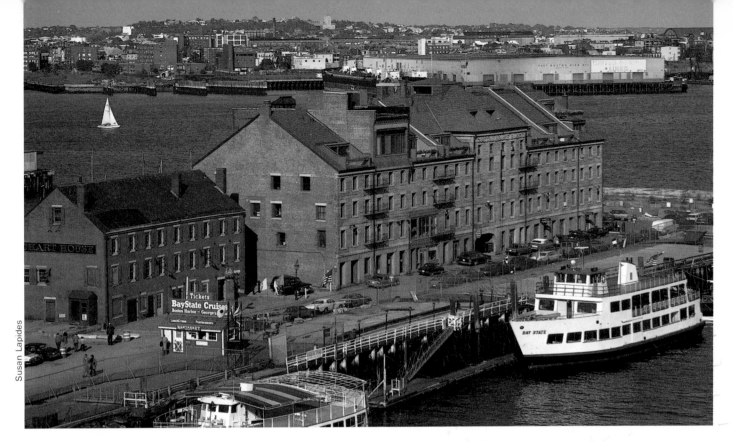

Boats of all kinds and sizes share the waters of the harbor.

cargo. Fishing boats weigh the day's catch on the piers as seagulls circle overhead. Since Logan Airport juts out into the middle of the harbor, airplanes and helicopters take off and land right over the water.

The ocean also plays a role in Boston's weather. East winds cool the land, and the sea breezes bring a strong salty smell into the city. Sometimes heavy fog rolls in and hides all the tall buildings from view. Yet the sea also helps keep the city warmer than inland areas during the winter.

When snow falls on other parts of New England, Boston often gets rain or sleet instead.

The busy waterfront seems quiet compared with the crowded streets. Other cities have streets laid out in a neat, crossing pattern, but not Boston. Four-lane highways loop around the city's edges while crooked, one-way streets zigzag through its center. Cars and trucks honk all day long as they try to make their way down the narrow, winding roads.

The streets were first built when people traveled by horse or on foot. Some of them are just alleys—barely wide enough for ox-carts to pass through, let alone cars. A few of Boston's streets are paved with cobblestones, put down many, many years ago. In some neighborhoods old-fashioned gaslights shine on the cobblestones and brick sidewalks.

To some people, Boston seems like a sea of bricks—from the vast plaza at City Hall and the gold-domed State House to the neighborhood townhouses of Beacon Hill and Back Bay. Yet, in the last thirty years, new offices and apartments have added other colors and textures to the city.

Today, towering skyscrapers of glass, concrete, and steel loom above the old buildings. The city's tallest buildings stand near Copley Square. Passing clouds are reflected in the Hancock Insurance building's glass walls. With sixty stories, it's the tallest building in New England.

Boston is not all buildings and

In the spring, magnolia blossoms brighten Boston's Back Bay area.

Clouds are reflected in the soaring glass walls of the Hancock building.

busy streets. In fact, it has more parks than many American cities. Together the parks, called the Emerald Necklace, are draped around the city like a string of jewels. Bostonians treasure the greenery. During the hot summer months, the parks fill with city workers eating their picnic lunches, children tossing Frisbees, bikers, roller skaters, runners, and people-watchers.

The Boston Common, the oldest public park in America, lies right in the middle of the city's busy downtown. When Boston was still a small fishing village in 1634, its citizens set aside this large field, where they kept their cows. Ben Franklin grazed his family's cow here. Later, when the city grew larger and busier, cows were banned from the Common.

Children play in the Boston Common.

Next to the Common at the Public Garden, majestic weeping willow trees shade the banks of the duck pond where the mallard family from *Make Way for Ducklings* lives. Bostonians and visitors enjoy a stroll through the Public Garden. They can feed the ducks or circle the pond in grand old swan boats. These green and red boats with giant swan heads glide quietly through the water, driven by pedal power rather than motors.

When it rains, or when snow

Colorful swan boats float in the pond at Boston's Public Garden.

blankets the ground, people turn indoors for entertainment. They might watch a dolphin show at the aquarium or a movie about the planets and the stars at the planetarium. Sports fans can watch the Celtics play basketball or the Bruins play hockey at the Boston Garden. Music lovers may go to the symphony or a musical. If they want to stay home, they can tune to one of the city's thirty-three radio or eight TV stations.

Bostonians can find just about any kind of museum, theater, library, or sports activity. In fact, in the 1800s, citizens called Boston the "hub of the universe" because they thought it was the center of culture and learning in America, even the world. Today Boston is still a hub. People come from around the world to study at its well-known universities. Computer companies, publishers, printers, insurance companies, and banks have their headquarters here.

Because Boston has so many different types of businesses, all types of people live and work in the city. Writers, artists, bus drivers, bankers, hotel workers, doctors, postal clerks, and engineers make Boston their home. Students form one of the largest groups. The city has twenty-five colleges, and these young people give the city added energy and excitement.

With its strong links to the past, Boston is a city that honors its history and traditions. Yet it is also a city of new ideas that looks toward the future. Even as it grows and changes, it preserves its centuries-old heritage.

2

Puritans, Rebels, and Presidents

Boston is often called the "home of the bean and the cod." Its nickname, "Beantown," has roots that go back to the first settlers of Boston, the Puritans. Thick and gooey baked beans were a common meal for the Puritans, who worked hard all week long and rested on the Sabbath when no cooking was done. On Saturday they prepared a pot of beans and let them bake overnight for Sunday's dinner.

Codfish, or "scrod," comes from the Atlantic coastal waters. Cod and beans, still popular today, are just a small part of Boston's rich past.

The Puritans who founded Boston in 1630 wanted to form a community where everyone shared their beliefs and each person had an equal say over the affairs of the government. Since they didn't get along with the Church of England, they came to

The 1795 American flag, with fifteen stars for the first fifteen U.S. states, flies aboard the USS *Constitution* in Boston's harbor.

America. In the new land they set up their own church, government, and school system, and held democratic town meetings. In the town meetings, every church member had an equal voice in making decisions. Today, town meetings continue to be an important part of local government in New England.

Because the Puritans wanted to live only with people who shared their religious beliefs, they drove away anyone who disagreed with them. They treated Quakers and other religious groups with different ideas as outcasts. Some Quakers were even hanged on the Common. The Puritans banished Roger Williams, who preached that everyone had a right to worship in his or her own way. He and his followers fled to Rhode Island.

During the 1700s, Boston grew and prospered. As time passed, many of the city's citizens came to believe that they should not have to follow the laws of England. In the period that led up to the American Revolution, they began to rebel against the British government.

In 1764 the English Parliament started a program to raise money from the colonies. They put taxes on tea and other common goods. The taxes angered the colonists. Because they had no representatives in Parliament, they thought the British had no right to tax them. The colonists said: "No taxation without representation." In answer to the protests, the

British government sent soldiers to patrol the streets and keep the peace. The townspeople called them "redcoats," or "lobster-backs," because of the color of their jackets.

On March 5, 1770, a mob of colonists attacked some British soldiers. The soldiers fired into the crowd, killing five men. Among the dead was Crispus Attucks, the first black man to die for American freedom. The Boston Massacre, as it was called, led many Americans to believe that British soldiers did not belong on American soil.

Three years later, on December 16, 1773, colonists met at Faneuil Hall to complain about the high taxes on tea. After the meeting, about ninety men disguised themselves as Amer-

On July 4 in Boston, modern-day "redcoats" dress up as British soldiers.

Susan Lapides

ican Indians. That night at Griffins Wharf, they boarded three British tea ships and tossed 342 chests of tea into the cold waters of Boston Harbor.

The Boston Tea Party made King George furious. To punish Boston, Parliament closed the port so that no ships could come in to trade. This act united more people against the British. Food and other goods poured into Boston from the countryside.

When King George sent troops to put down the rebels, the colonists began to arm themselves. They believed that they had to protect their rights, by force if necessary. On April 18, 1775, two lights were hung in the steeple of the Old North Church. The lights signaled that the British army was coming by sea to Concord and Lexington to take away the patriots' arms and ammunition. Paul Revere, one of the patriots at the Tea Party, and two other men rode to Lexington and on to Concord to warn the citizens.

The farmers who formed the local military forces were known as minutemen because they had to be ready at a minute's notice. On Lexington Common the minutemen met the British and fired the first shot of the revolution—"the shot heard round the world." Later that day in Concord, they fought and won the first battle of the Revolution. The patriots chased the British all along the road back to Boston.

On June 17, 1775, another major

Balloons float in front of Faneuil Hall.

Robert Davis

battle took place in Charlestown—the battle of Bunker Hill. One story about the battle says that Colonel William Prescott, commander of the American forces, ordered his men: "Don't fire until you see the whites of their eyes." Though the patriots lost the battle when they ran out of gunpowder, the British suffered heavy losses.

Today a path called the Freedom Trail marks many of the famous sites from the Revolution. Visitors can see the Old North Church, Faneuil Hall, the Boston Tea Party Ship, the site of the Boston Massacre, and the house where Paul Revere lived with his wife and sixteen children.

Another historic path—the Black Heritage Trail on Beacon Hill—recalls

The Old North Church.

Paul Revere lived with his wife and sixteen children in this house.

a later period in the city's history. It marks many sites from the 1800s, when people began to speak out against slavery. The New England Antislavery Society was formed in Boston in 1832. Crowds at Faneuil Hall heard speeches protesting slavery. Slowly, the city's citizens began to respond.

They set up the underground railroad, made up of places where escaped slaves could stay as they fled north to freedom. Many homes on Beacon Hill served as safe way stations for black Americans trying to reach Canada. During this period, the African Meeting House, the first black church in America, was built on Joy Street. Later, two troops of black soldiers from Massachusetts fought in the Civil War on the Union side. At the war's end, Boston celebrated the Union victory with a grand Peace Jubilee.

In 1872 a great fire swept through downtown Boston, destroying hundreds of businesses. The city was quickly rebuilt, and its population grew rapidly.

In the twentieth century, two Boston men served the nation as president. In 1919, during Calvin Coolidge's term as mayor, Boston's police officers went on strike. When mobs looted the unprotected city, Coolidge had to call in the National Guard to protect the peace. He gained national fame and became president in 1923.

In 1960 Americans elected John Fitzgerald Kennedy as the thirty-fifth president of the United States. President Kennedy was born in Brookline, just outside Boston. People throughout the United States and the world mourned when Kennedy was shot and killed in Dallas, Texas, on November 22, 1963. A memorial to the president, the John Fitzgerald Kennedy Library and Museum, opened to the public in 1979.

Today, Boston faces many of the same issues that other cities do. Its local government has worked to solve problems of crime, rundown neigh-

The John Fitzgerald Kennedy Library.

borhoods, unemployment, and poverty. Over the last thirty years, a plan to improve the city's living and working conditions has made life better for many Bostonians. New hotels and office buildings have changed the skyline in just a few years. More business has meant more jobs, too. With its new buildings and businesses, Boston builds toward a bright future.

3

The Neighborhoods

Since the American Revolution, people from many nations have come to Boston. Irish, Italian, Chinese, British, Russian, and Greek immigrants have settled in separate parts of the city. Today, Boston's neighborhoods are so different from one another that some people think of them as separate towns.

The North End, the city's oldest neighborhood, has narrow, winding streets and four-story brick apartment houses. Most of the families are descendants of Italian immigrants who settled here between 70 and 100 years ago. No one has a yard in the North End. On warm evenings neighbors often set up chairs on the sidewalk and chat with passersby. Children play ball in the quiet streets. Along the waterfront, old warehouses have been made into comfortable

Crowded, narrow, winding streets run through the neighborhoods of Boston.

apartments and condominiums. Still, a few wharves support old-time businesses like the Bay State Lobster Company.

Most of the Italian families are Roman Catholic and celebrate religious traditions and Italian customs with festivals during the summer. Garlands decorate the streets, which are marked off with arches. Raffles, games, food, music, and parades highlight the celebrations. At the Fisherman's Festival in August, young girls dress up as angels. One girl is lowered from a balcony to the street and gives a speech in Italian. Then doves fly out of a cage as confetti drifts down from the sky.

A big shopping market lies near the North End. For more than 300 years, local farmers have been bringing their fresh fruits and vegetables to Haymarket. They sell their goods at outdoor stalls along the edge of the highway. People come from all over the city to buy fresh oranges and apples, Vermont cheeses, and many other tasty foods.

A quieter section of the city, Beacon Hill, borders the Boston Common. At the very top of the hill stands the State House and other government offices. Elegant brick townhouses and small apartment buildings line the lower slopes. Old-fashioned gaslights shine on the steep, narrow cobblestone streets.

Many famous Boston families have lived on Beacon Hill. Louisa May Alcott, who wrote *Little Women*,

People come from all over the city to buy fresh fruits and vegetables at Haymarket.

had a home on Louisburg Square. At Christmastime wreaths and ribbons decorate the doorways and lamp posts in the square. Carolers come from all over the city to join in the singing and listen to the Beacon Hill Hand Bell Ringers Band.

During the late 1800s many families moved from Beacon Hill to Back Bay, where grand brick townhouses and apartments were built. Back Bay once was the back bay of the Charles River, a polluted, smelly place. The townspeople decided to fill in the

Acorn Street is one of the steep, narrow, cobble-stone streets on Beacon Hill.

mud flats and create a new neighborhood with broad, tree-lined avenues.

Part of Back Bay is a big shopping district. Cafés, art galleries, and clothing stores flank Newbury Street. Shoppers and office workers scurry in and out of nearby Copley Square and Copley Place shopping mall. Because of the lively nightlife in the area, many young working people and students like to live in Back Bay.

Nearer the center of the city, a giant gate with green roof tiles and lions marks the entrance to Chinatown. This neighborhood has pagoda-shaped phone booths and Chinese street signs. Many of its residents and shopkeepers speak Chinese as their first language. Visitors like to shop at the small Chinese markets, where

Brick townhouses line the broad, tree-lined avenues of Back Bay.

This gate marks the entrance to Boston's Chinatown.

they can buy bamboo leaves, dried shrimp, and all sorts of noodles.

Chinatown has some of the city's most colorful festivals. The Chinese New Year's celebrations begin with a dragon and lion dance. The August Moon Festival, held when the moon is full, is much like the American Thanksgiving. People gather for a lion dance, folk dancing, and singing. Food stands sell moon cakes.

Of the many ethnic groups in Boston, the Irish are the largest. Many families left Ireland during a potato

famine in the 1840s and settled in South Boston. Today the area still has strong family and neighborhood ties. Those Irish ties stand out on Saint Patrick's Day when proud "Southies" celebrate with a big parade.

While the residents of South Boston are called "Southies," the citizens of East Boston are known as "Easties." To reach East Boston, people drive through the Callahan Tunnel under the harbor. In this area, many Italian and Asian families live in wooden row houses and triple decker apartments. Logan Airport is located in East Boston.

A bridge connects Charlestown to Boston. Bunker Hill Monument towers over this hilly section of the city. Young working people like to live near the Charlestown waterfront so that they can walk to downtown offices.

Roxbury, Dorchester, and Jamaica Plain are neighborhoods on the southern side of the city, where many black and Hispanic families live. The residents take pride in their neighborhood. They support many churches, theaters, and social action groups.

Roxbury hosts a Caribbean Carnival Festival in August. The loud music of bands and steel drums echoes through the streets, and everyone dresses up in fantastic costumes. Of the many parks in this area, the most well known is Jamaica Plain's Arnold Arboretum. Hundreds of evergreens and flowering and hardwood trees grow here. In May, when the lilacs

bloom, people from neighborhoods all over the city meet on the paths of the arboretum.

From the North End to Beacon Hill, from Back Bay to Chinatown, from South Boston to Roxbury, each of Boston's neighborhoods has a character of its own. Yet they all fit together to form the complete picture of the big city.

The Ride of the Freedom Trail around Bunker Hill Monument in Charlestown.

4

From Yankee Traders to Computers

Modern-day Boston is a center of commerce, industry, finance, and medicine. It is a major East Coast port, an important fish market, and the largest wool market in the United States.

The city's early residents made their living from the sea. The greatest days of the port were in the 1800s when ship captains and merchants such as George Cabot became rich through the "China trade." From Boston, fast clipper ships sailed around Cape Horn to the Pacific Coast, where they bought furs to sell in Hawaii, China, and Russia. They loaded their ships with silk, tea, and other goods from the Far East to sell on their return. The great age of the clipper ships ended soon after the invention of steam-powered vessels.

When shipping declined, busi-

Skyscrapers in modern-day Boston rise along the Charles River.

ness people turned to manufacturing. In the 1800s, Boston became an industrial center. Francis Cabot Lowell invented the power loom, and he built the city's first cotton and textile mills.

The textile mills closed long ago, but today many people work in factories producing women's sportswear and other clothing. Retail clothing stores are important, too. The two biggest, Jordan Marsh and Filene's, have branches all over New England. Elizabeth Taylor and other show business stars have shopped at Filene's famous bargain basement.

Printing and publishing are the city's largest manufacturing industries. *The News-Letter*, the first regular newspaper to be published in America, was started in Boston in 1704. Today Bostonians get their news from the city's two major dailies, the *Boston Globe* and the *Herald*. People the world over read the *Christian Science Monitor*, a highly respected international daily newspaper. Books are another important Boston product. Writers, editors, printers, and art directors pool their talents at the city's large book publishing companies. Local companies create many of the textbooks used by students in American classrooms.

Many skilled doctors, nurses, researchers, and others in health care work at Boston's hospitals. The city is one of the major medical research centers in the United States. People come from all over the country, and even from the Soviet Union and Japan, for treatment in Boston.

Many of the medical centers have close ties with the city's universities. Education has always held an important place in Boston, starting with the Puritans. In 1635, only five years after they arrived, they founded the Boston Latin School. This marked the beginning of the American public school system. Today, students still attend Boston Latin School, which accepts outstanding pupils from all over the city.

Harvard College, America's first university, was founded by the Puritans in 1636 to educate young people in "knowledge and godliness." Located on the river in Cambridge, Harvard is one of the most famous uni-

The offices of the *Christian Science Monitor* are located in the Christian Science Church Center near downtown Boston.

Harvard University lies just across the Charles River from Boston.

versities in the world. Among its graduates are well-known government leaders, writers, scientists, and doctors. Presidents Franklin Delano Roosevelt and John F. Kennedy studied here.

Just down the road from Harvard is the Massachusetts Institute of Technology, which is known for its excellence in the sciences. Nobel Prize winners in economics, chemistry, and physics teach here. Other universities in the Boston area include Tufts University, Boston College, and Northeastern University, the first American community college. Martin Luther King, Jr., attended Boston University, the first American university to admit women on equal terms with men.

Boston's universities and research centers have helped create new businesses and jobs. Scientists and researchers came up with the ideas that led to the success of many computer and other high-technology companies. Polaroid, Wang, Digital, Data General, and other companies have led the way in developing equipment for space research. Their computers and software (computer programs) are used by businesses everywhere.

Route 128, a highway that loops around the city, is called America's High Technology Region because so many of these companies are clustered here. In the future, many new jobs will be created in the high-technology field. Boston's universities will train young people for these jobs as engineers, scientists, and computer programmers. In this way they will help the city's businesses meet the challenges of the twenty-first century.

5

Fun and Entertainment

How do Bostonians entertain themselves when they have a holiday from school or a day off from work? In the museums they can explore many exciting subjects. The Museum of Science draws huge crowds. Visitors may see a skeleton of a dinosaur or climb inside a space capsule and imagine what it's like to be an astronaut. At this museum the Hayden Planetarium shows programs about the solar system, and the Omni Theater runs exciting nature movies on a giant screen.

Other museums appeal to special groups. In the Children's Museum, exhibits explain such things as how the different parts of the body work. At the Computer Museum, visitors experiment with different computer programs to find out what it's like to fly a plane or to create a special melody.

Children touch a lifelike dinosaur at the Museum of Science.

A girl gets a close-up look at fish from around the world at the New England Aquarium.

Marine life is on display at the New England Aquarium, where a spiral staircase surrounds a giant fish tank—three stories high! Sharks, sea turtles, and moray eels swim inside the thick glass walls. At the aquarium, people may board a ship and go on a whale-watching trip to George's Bank on the Atlantic Ocean. In these waters, huge humpback and pilot whales feed on tiny sea creatures called plankton.

The USS *Constitution*, the oldest ship on active duty in the U.S. Navy, ranks as nearly everyone's favorite "museum." Launched in Boston in 1797, it was supposed to be the finest warship ever built. "Old Ironsides" received its nickname during a battle in the War of 1812 because cannon-balls bounced off its thick oak planks. Today the ship stays at its berth in Charlestown Navy Yard so that people can climb aboard and see how warships were built nearly two hundred years ago.

To find out more about how the world is put together, children may visit the Mapparium, a bright, stained glass globe of the world at the Christian Science Center. A bridge leads inside the globe and into the center of the earth. The giant globe shows different land surfaces and ocean depths.

The USS *Constitution* in the Charlestown Navy Yard.

Clocks tell the time for other parts of the world.

Children who enjoy music, theater, or dance can find plenty of activities to entertain them. On the Fourth of July, the Boston Pops orchestra gives a concert at the Hatch Shell on the Esplanade. Thousands attend to hear the music and watch the fireworks. In the winter, the Boston Symphony plays at Symphony Hall.

Popular puppet shows like *The Three Bears* and *Beauty and the Beast* entertain children and adults at the Puppet Showplace Theatre. Students from the Boston Children's Theatre School put on plays during the school year. The theatre school is a special school for boys and girls skilled in creative drama. One of the most be-loved shows of the year is performed by the Boston Ballet. *The Nutcracker Suite* delights young and old every year during the Christmas holidays.

Boston's sports fans enjoy baseball, basketball, hockey, and even a foot race that takes more than two hours to run. The Boston Marathon, the oldest marathon in the country, has been held every year since 1897. Patriot's Day, the third Monday in April, is a school holiday, and most businesses are closed for the big race. Thousands of Bostonians turn out to cheer on the 7,000 to 8,000 runners. The race starts in the town of Hopkinton and leads more than twenty-six miles into Copley Square. Former winners include Joan Benoit Samuelson, the first woman to win the gold

At the Christian Science Center Mapparium, a giant globe provides visitors with a lesson in world geography.

medal for the marathon in the Olympic Games.

The Boston Red Sox, another Boston legend, start their season in the spring. Though the Red Sox haven't won the World Series since 1918, hope never seems to die. Whether their team is winning or losing, Boston fans fill the stands at old Fenway Park. Famous Red Sox hitters such as Ted Williams, Carl "Yaz" Yastrzemski, and Wade Boggs have tested their batting skills against the Green Monster, the tall left-field wall.

Boston Garden is home for two teams, the Boston Bruins and the Celtics. Bobby Orr helped the Bruins win hockey's Stanley Cup during the 1970s. Because Boston has so many Irish men and women, the owner of its basketball team named it the Celtics and put the players in green suits. Superstars in the "green machine's" lineup have included Bob Cousy, Bill Russell, John Havlicek, Dave Cowens, and Larry Bird.

Boston takes pride in its superstars. Sports heroes, U.S. presidents, great writers, and inventors have all had important roles in making the city an exciting center for people to live, work, and play. And the people, both past and present, have been the city's greatest strength.

Boston Red Sox star Wade Boggs takes a swing during a game in Fenway Park.

Places to Visit in Boston

Alexander Graham Bell's Garret
New England Telephone Headquarters Building
185 Franklin Street
Workshop where Bell invented the telephone

Boston Common
Visitor Information Center
Tremont Street
Freedom Trail starting point

Boston Garden
150 Causeway Street
(617) 227-3200

Boston Massacre Site
Old State House, 206 Washington Street
(617) 242-5619

Boston Tea Party Ship and Museum
Congress Street Bridge
(617) 338-1773

Bunker Hill Pavilion
55 Constitution Road, Charlestown
(617) 241-7575
Multi-media show on the Battle of Bunker Hill

Children's Museum
300 Congress Street, Museum Wharf
(617) 426-6500

Christian Science Center/Mapparium
1 Norway Street
(617) 450-3790

Christian Science Center Publishing House
175 Huntington Avenue
(617) 450-3790
Tours of the building where the Christian Science Monitor and other periodicals are published.

Computer Museum
300 Congress Street, Museum Wharf
(617) 423-6758

Faneuil Hall
Congress Street/Faneuil Hall Marketplace
(617) 725-3105

Fenway Park
4 Yawkey Way
(617) 267-8661

John Fitzgerald Kennedy Library
Columbia Point on Dorchester Bay
(617) 929-4523

John Hancock Observatory
200 Clarendon Street, Copley Square
(617) 247-1976

Metropolitan Boston Zoo
Franklin Park
(617) 442-0991

Museum of Fine Arts Boston
465 Huntington Avenue
(617) 267-9300

Museum of Science
Science Park
(617) 742-6088
Includes the Omni Theater and the Hayden Planetarium

New England Aquarium
Central Wharf
(617) 742-8870
Whale watch information: (617) 973-5277

Old North Church
193 Salem Street, North End
(617) 523-6676

Old South Meeting House
310 Washington Street
(617) 482-6439

Paul Revere House
19 North Square, North End
(617) 523-1676

Puppet Showplace Theatre
32 Station Street, Brookline
(617) 731-6400

The Skywalk
50th Floor Observation Deck
800 Boylston Street, Prudential Tower
(617) 236-3318

Symphony Hall
301 Massachusetts Avenue
(617) 266-1200

USS Constitution Museum
Charlestown Navy Yard
(617) 426-1812

Additional information can be obtained from these agencies:

Bostonian Society
Old State House
206 Washington Street
Boston, Massachusetts 02109
(617) 242-5619

Greater Boston Convention and Visitors Bureau, Inc.
Prudential Plaza   P.O. Box 490
Boston, Massachusetts 02199
(617) 536-4100

Massachusetts Department of Tourism and Development
100 Cambridge Street
Boston, Massachusetts 02202
(617) 727-3201

National Park Service
15 State Street
Boston, Massachusetts 02109
(617) 242-5642

Boston: A Historical Time Line

1630   A group of Puritans found Boston on the Shawmut Peninsula

1632   Boston becomes the capital of Massachusetts Bay Colony

1635   Boston Latin School, the first public school in America, opens

1636   Harvard College is founded

1639   The first post office in America opens in Boston

1692-93   19 people are killed and about 150 imprisoned on charges of witchcraft during the Salem Witch Trials

1704   First American newspaper, *The Boston News-Letter*, is published

1742   Peter Faneuil builds Faneuil Hall as a public market and meeting place for the people of Boston

1770   British soldiers fire into a rioting crowd in the Boston Massacre

1773   Patriots stage the Boston Tea Party to protest high tea taxes

1775   Paul Revere rides through the Massachusetts countryside to warn colonists that "The British are coming!"

1797   John Adams becomes president

1822   Boston is chartered as a city

1825   John Quincy Adams becomes president

1832   New England Antislavery Society is formed in Boston

1854   Boston Public Library, first public library in America, is established

1872   The Great Fire destroys 776 buildings in downtown Boston

1879   Mary Baker Eddy establishes the Church of Christ, Scientist

1897   First Boston Marathon is held

1897   Boston is first American city to have a subway as the Tremont Street subway opens

1904	The nation's first underwater mass transit tunnel, the East Boston Tunnel, opens	1975	Boston desegregates its public schools by order of a federal court
1919	Violence erupts throughout the city during the Boston Police Strike	1980s	Boston experiences an economic boom based on its growing high-tech industries
1923	Calvin Coolidge becomes president	1988	Michael Dukakis is the Democratic candidate for president
1961	John F. Kennedy becomes president		

Index